JUST FOR FUN

ROCK AND POP BANJO

12 GREAT SONGS FROM CLASSIC TO MODERN ROCK

ARRANGED BY ANDREW DUBROCK

Produced by
Alfred Music Publishing Co., Inc.
P.O. Box 10003
Van Nuys, CA 91410-0003
alfred.com

Printed in USA.

ISBN-10: 0-7390-6467-3
ISBN-13: 978-0-7390-6467-2

Cover Photos
Central image models: Katrina Hruschka and Andrew Callahan / Photographer: Brian Immke, www.adeptstudios.com
Mastertone banjo: courtesy of Gibson USA • Moon: courtesy of The Library of Congress • Gramophone: © istockphoto / Faruk Tasdemir
MP3 player: © istockphoto / tpopova • Microphone: © istockphoto / Graffizone • Handstand: © istockphoto / jhorrocks
Jumping woman: © istockphoto / Dan Wilton • Woman and radio: courtesy of The Library of Congress • Sneakers: © istockphoto / ozgurdonmaz
Background: image copyright Elise Gravel, 2009, used under license from Shutterstock.com

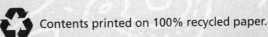

Contents printed on 100% recycled paper.

FOREWORD

Rock and Pop Banjo is designed for your total enjoyment. Each song uses the original guitar parts arranged for the banjo, but in some cases we've elaborated on the arrangement with banjo roll patterns. Make sure to listen to the original recordings so you know how the parts should sound before you start trying to learn them. But most important, just have fun!

—Aaron Stang, Editor
Alfred Music Publishing Co., Inc.

CONTENTS

BEAT IT

Tune down 1/2 step to match recording:

⑤ = G♭   ② = B♭
④ = D♭   ① = D♭
③ = G♭

Written and Composed by
MICHAEL JACKSON

Moderately fast ♩ = 136

Intro:

1. They told him don't you ev - er   come a - round   here.   Don't
2. They're out to get you, bet - ter   leave while you   can.   Don't

Optional picking pattern (and riff pattern) throughout

6

— 'em how funk-y, strong__ is your fight. It____ does-n't mat-ter, who's__

1.

w/Rhy. Fig. 1 *simile*

__ wrong or right. Just beat it, beat it. Just beat it, beat it. Just

2.

w/Rhy. Fig. 1 *(2 times) simile*

beat it, beat it. Just beat it, beat it. Ooh. beat it, beat it, beat it, beat it. No__

__ one wants to be de-feat-ed. Show__ 'em how funk-y, strong__ is your fight. It__

__ does-n't mat-ter, who's__wrong or right. Just beat it, beat it, beat it. Beat it, beat it.

Beat it, beat it. Beat it, beat it.

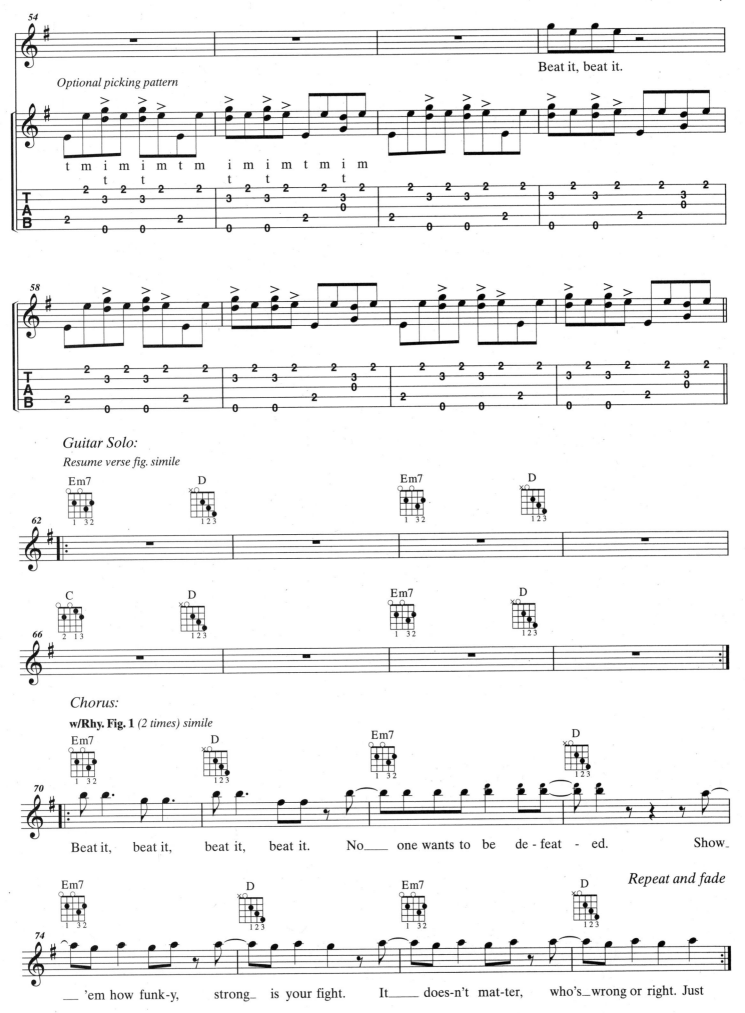

CHINA GROVE

Words and Music by
TOM JOHNSTON

10

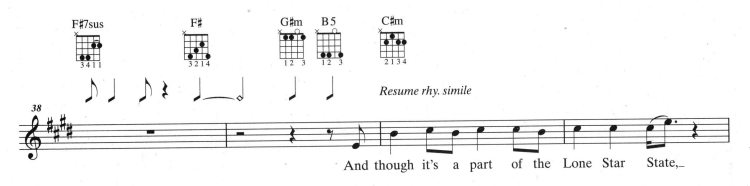

Resume rhy. simile

And though it's a part of the Lone Star State,

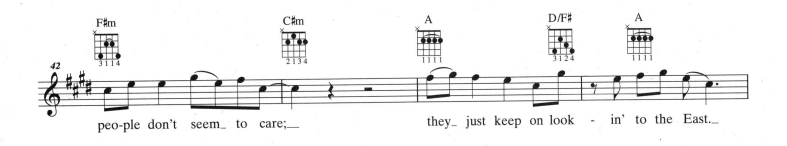

peo-ple don't seem_ to care;_ they_ just keep on look - in' to the East._

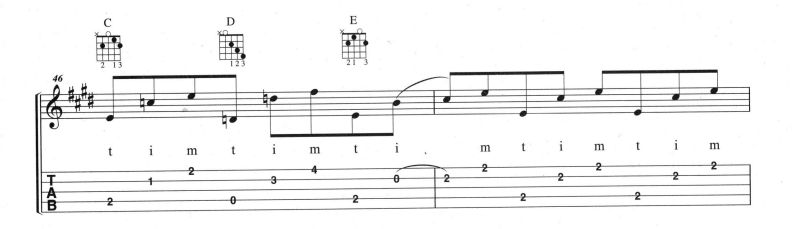

D.C. al Fine
(with repeats)

DO YOU WANT TO KNOW A SECRET

Slowly

Intro:

Words and Music by
JOHN LENNON and PAUL McCARTNEY

You'll nev - er know how much I real - ly love you.

Moderately fast

You'll nev - er know how much I real - ly care.

Verse:

Optional picking pattern for Verse

Lis-ten, do you want to know a se - cret?

Cont. rhy. simile

do you prom-ise not to tell? Woah. Clos-er,

Do You Want to Know a Secret - 2 - 1

DON'T STOP BELIEVIN'

Moderately ♩ = 120

Intro:

Words and Music by
JONATHAN CAIN, NEAL SCHON
and STEVE PERRY

*See Verse for optional picking pattern.

Verse 1:

Just a small town girl,___ liv-in' in a lone-ly world.___

Optional picking pattern for Verse

She took the mid-night train_ go-in' an - y - where.___

Don't Stop Believin' - 4 - 1

JUMPIN' JACK FLASH

Words and Music by
MICK JAGGER and KEITH RICHARDS

20

Interlude:

hold throughout

I was drowned,

Verse 3:

w/Rhy. Fig. 1 *(4 times), simile*

I was washed_ up and left_ for dead._____ I fell_ down_

_____ to my feet_ and I saw_ they bled._____ I frowned_

at the crumbs_ of a crust_ of bread._____ I was crowned_

_____ with a spike_ right thru my_ head._____ Ah,___ ah yeah._ But it's all_

Chorus:

Resume chorus fig. simile

_____ right now, in fact, it's a gas!____ ____ But it's all_____

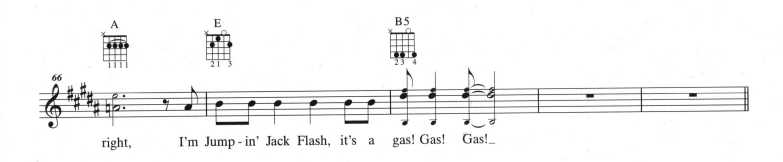

right, I'm Jump - in' Jack Flash, it's a gas! Gas! Gas!_

Outro:

Repeat and fade

(Jump-in' Jack Flash, it's a gas!_ Jump - in' Jack Flash, it's a gas!_)

(enter 3rd time)

t i m t i m t i m m i m i t i t i t i t i m t i m t i m m i m i t i t i

LAYLA
(*Unplugged* version)

Words and Music by
ERIC CLAPTON and JIM GORDON

LYIN' EYES

Moderately fast ♩ = 132

Intro:

Words and Music by
DON HENLEY and GLENN FREY

Lyin' Eyes - 4 - 1

Verse 3:
So she tells him she must go out for the evening
To comfort an old friend who's feeling down.
But he knows where she's going as she's leaving.
She is headed for the cheating side of town.
(To Chorus:)

Verse 4:
On the other side of town a boy is waiting
With fiery eyes and dreams no one could steal.
She drives on through the night anticipating,
'Cause he makes her feel the way she used to feel.

Verse 5:
She rushes to his arms, they fall together
She whispers that it's only for a while.
She swears that soon she'll be coming back forever,
She pulls away and leaves him with a smile.
(To Chorus:)

Verse 6:
She gets up and pours herself a strong one,
And stares out at the stars up in the sky.
Another night it's gonna be a long one,
She draws the shade and hangs her head to cry.

Verse 7:
She wonders how it ever got this crazy.
She thinks about a boy she knew in school.
Did she get tired or did she just get lazy?
She's so far gone she feels just like a fool.

Verse 8:
My, oh, my, you sure know how to arrange things,
You set it up so well, so carefully
Ain't it funny how your new life didn't change things,
You're still the same old girl you used to be.
(To Chorus:)

PANAMA

*Tune down 1/2 step to match recording:

⑤ = G♭ ② = B♭
④ = D♭ ① = D♭
③ = G♭

Moderate rock ♩ = 144

Intro:

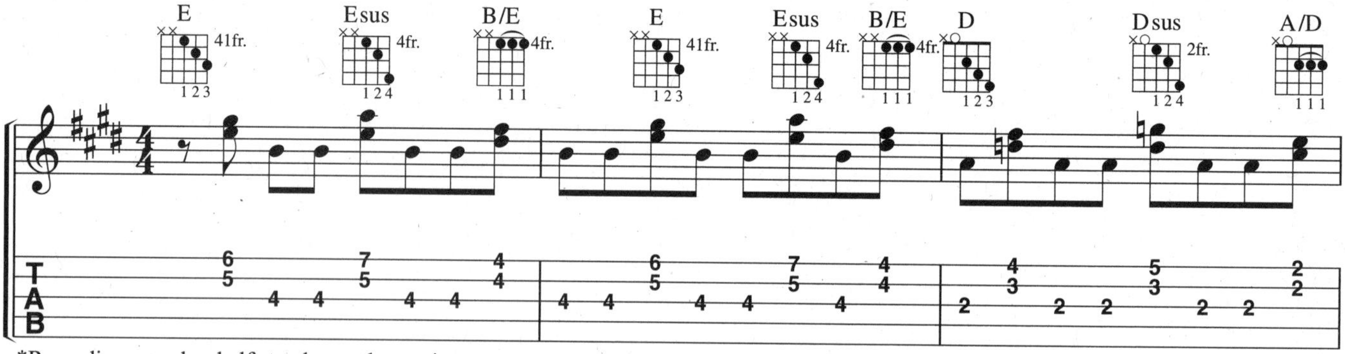

Words and Music by
EDWARD VAN HALEN, ALEX VAN HALEN,
MICHAEL ANTHONY and DAVID LEE ROTH

*Recording sounds a half step lower than written.

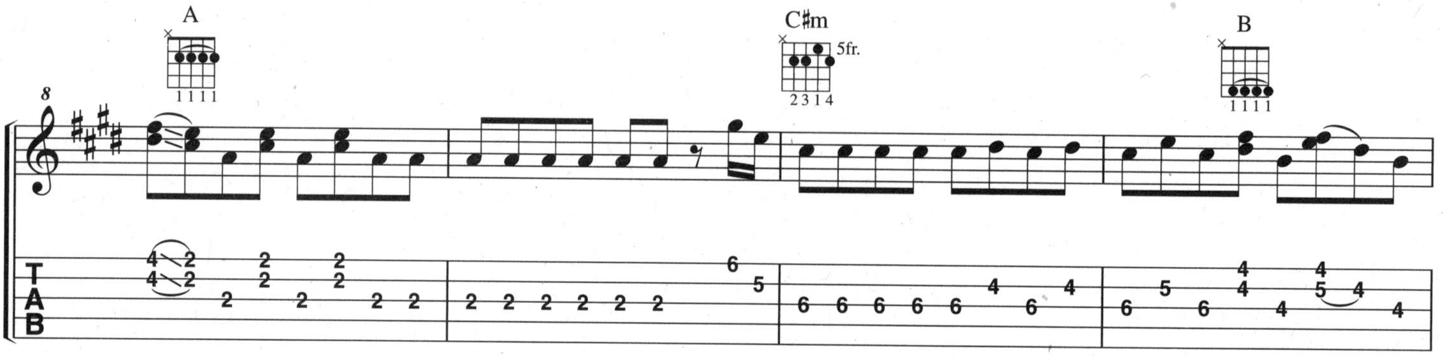

Panama - 6 - 1

Pan - a - ma,____   Pan - a - ma.____

____   ____ Ah oh____ oh oh____

Instrumental Solo (ad lib.):

____ oh.

Bridge:

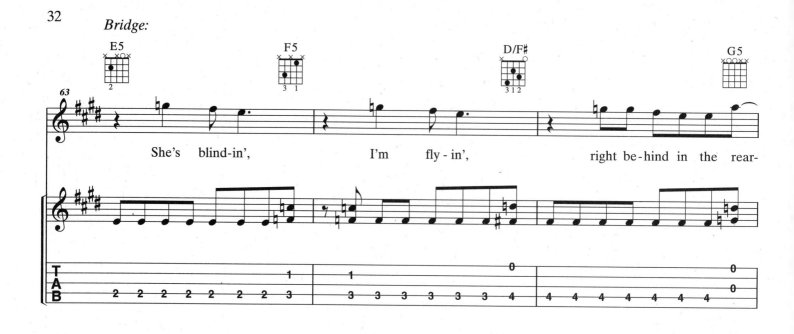

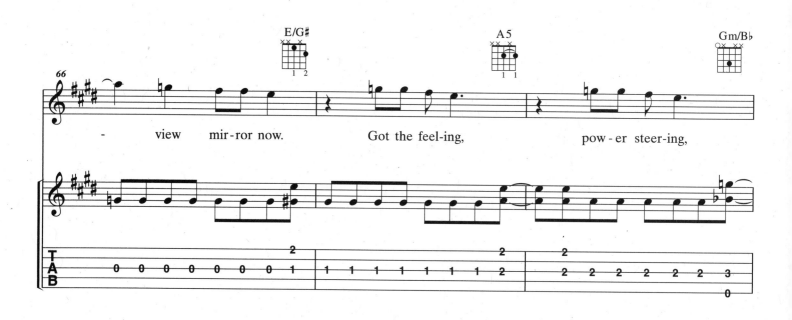

Outro Chorus:
w/Rhy. Fig. 1, *6 times, simile*

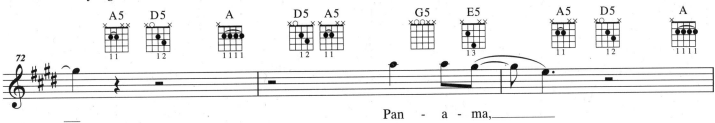

Pan - a - ma,_____

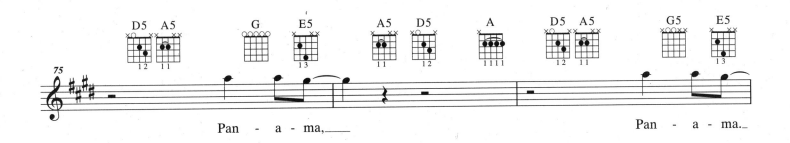

Pan - a - ma,____   Pan - a - ma._

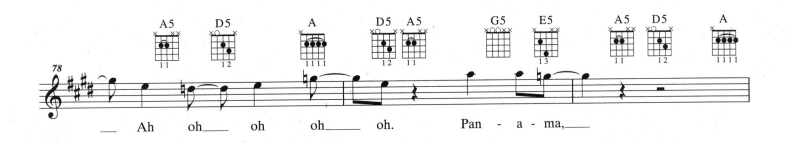

__ Ah oh__ oh oh__ oh.   Pan - a - ma,__

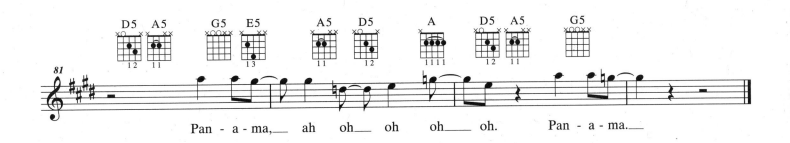

Pan - a - ma,__ ah oh__ oh oh__ oh.   Pan - a - ma._

Verse 2:
Ain't nothin' like it, her shiny machine,
Got the feel for the wheel, keep the moving parts clean.
Hot shoe, burnin' down the avenue,
Got an on-ramp comin' through my bedroom.
Don't you know she's comin' home to me?
You'll lose her in the turn.
I'll get her!
(To Chorus:)

HOW YOU REMIND ME

Lyrics by
CHAD KROEGER
Music by
NICKELBACK

How You Remind Me - 3 - 1

36

RUNNING ON EMPTY

Moderately fast ♩ = 146

Words and Music by
JACKSON BROWNE

1. Look-ing out at the road___ rush-ing un-der my wheels.___
2.3. *See additional lyrics*

Look-ing back at the years___ gone by___ like so___ man-y sum-mer fields.___

Six-ty five, I was___ sev-en-teen,___ and run-ning up___ one-o-one.

Running on Empty - 5 - 1

38

Run-ning in-to the sun_____ but I'm run-ning be-hind.____

Outro:

Resume Verse rhy. simile

Play 6 times

Lead Gtr. *(arr. for banjo)*

(3rd & 5th time only)

rit.

Verse 2:
Gotta do what you can just to keep your love alive.
Tryin' not to confuse and with what you do to survive.
Sixty-nine, I was twenty-one, and I called the road my own.
I don't know when that road turned on to be the road I'm on.
(To Chorus:)

Verse 3:
Looking out at the road rushing under my wheels.
I don't know how to tell you all just how crazy this life feels.
I look around for the friends that I used to turn to, to pull me through.
Looking into their eyes, I see them running too.
(To Chorus:)

WILD NIGHT

Moderately fast ♩ = 152

Words and Music by
VAN MORRISON

STAYIN' ALIVE

Words and Music by
BARRY GIBB, MAURICE GIBB
and ROBIN GIBB

Moderately ♩ = 102

Intro:

Stayin' Alive - 3 - 1

48

1.

w/Rhy. Fig. 1

Fm

2.

w/Rhy. Fig. 1

Fm

26

2. Well, now I___

Bridge:

B♭7

Resume intro fig. simile (use riff from either B♭7 or Fm chord on intro) or Verse picking pattern

30

Life go - in' no - where,___ some-bod - y help me,___ some-bod - y help_me, yeah._

Fm

B♭7

33

___ Life go-in' no - where,___ some-bod - y help_me, yeah._

Fm

D.S. 𝄋 al Coda

37

___ I'm stay-in' a - live.___ 3. Well, you can tell_

✠ *Coda*

w/Rhy. Fig. 1

Fm

Bridge:

B♭7

Resume Bridge fig. or picking pattern simile

40

Life go-in' no - where,___ some-bod-y help me,___

Fm

B♭7

44

some - bod - y help_me, yeah.___ Life go-in' no -where,___

Fm

Repeat ad lib. and fade

48

some-bod-y help_me, yeah.___ I'm stay-in' a - live.___

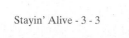

Stayin' Alive - 3 - 3

BANJO CHORD DICTIONARY

A CHORDS

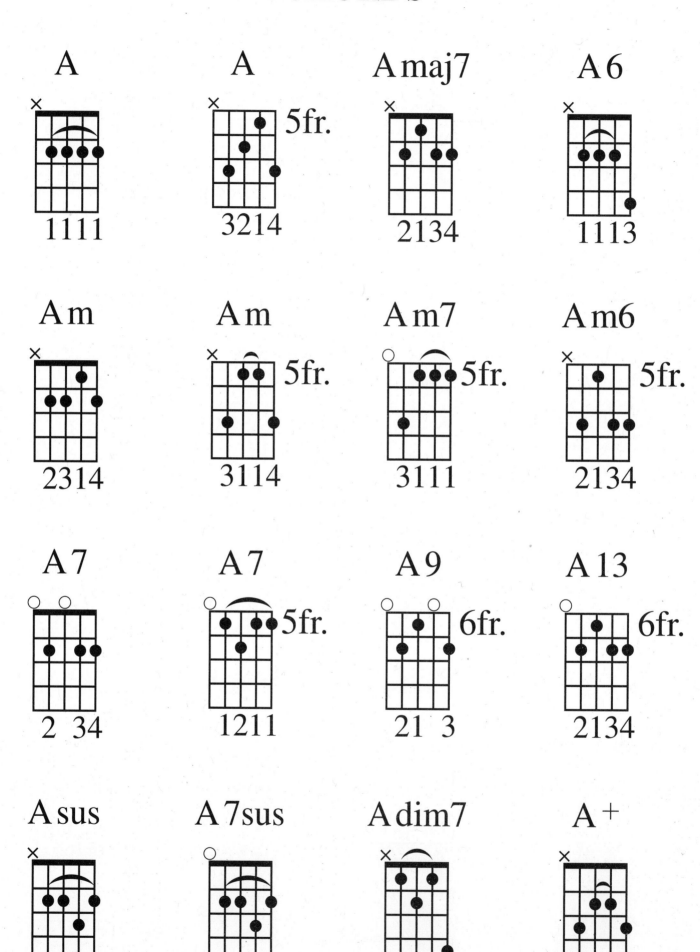

B♭ (A♯) CHORDS*

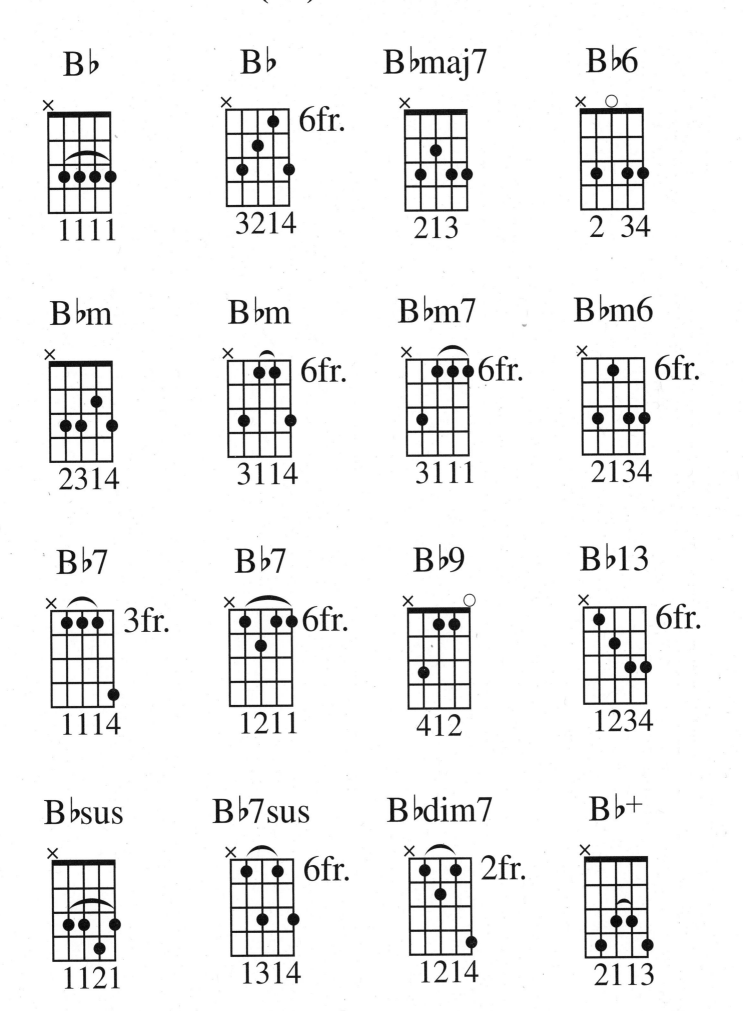

*B♭ and A♯ are two names for the same note.

B CHORDS

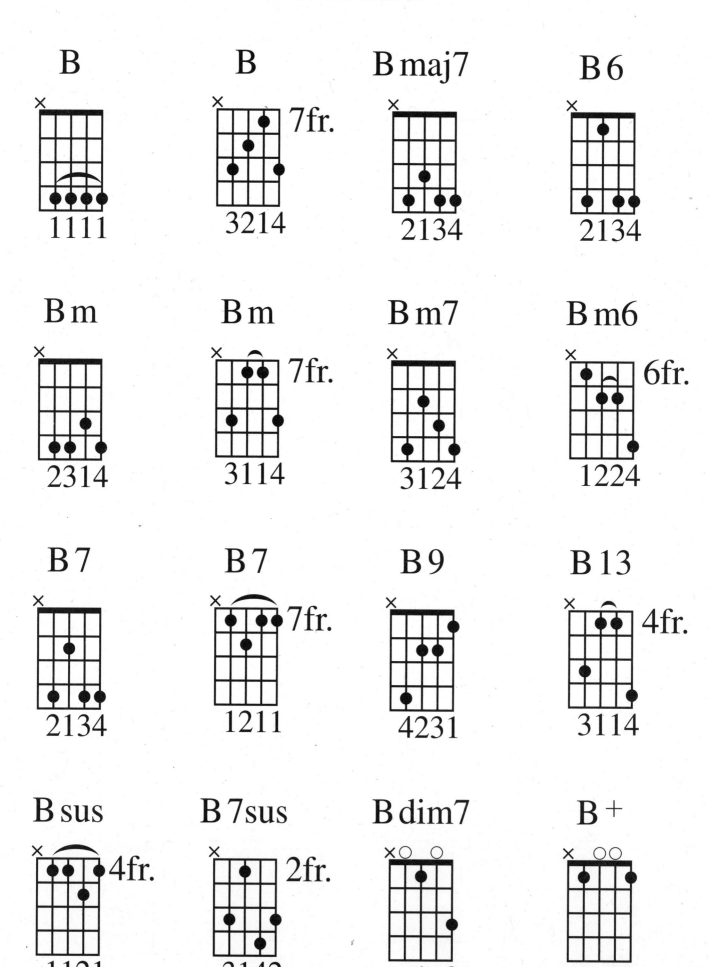

C CHORDS

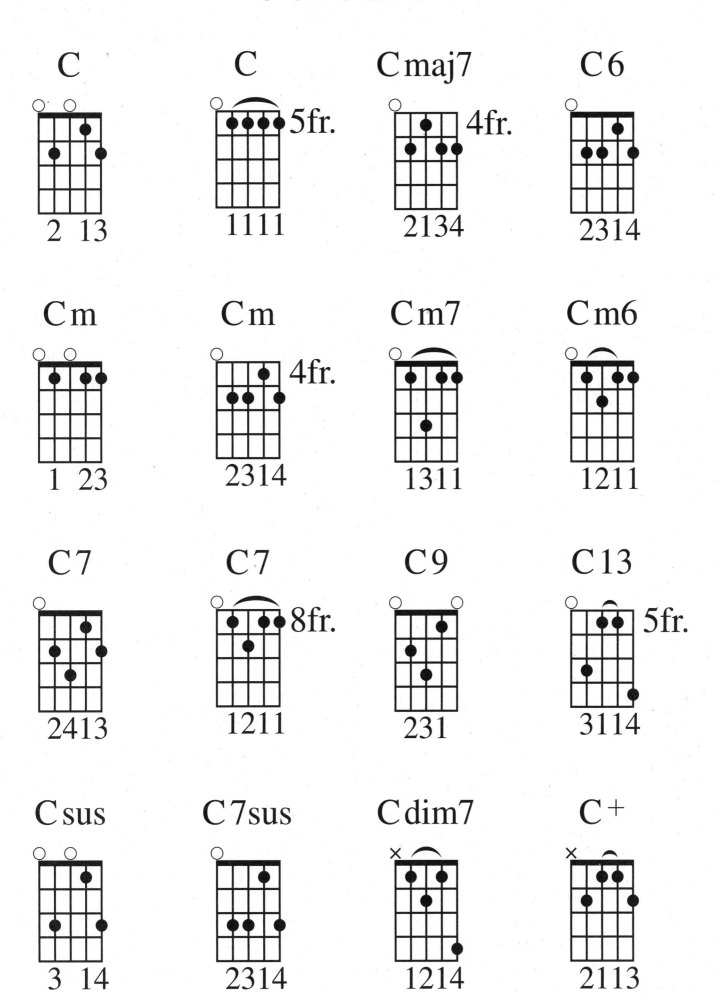

C♯ (D♭) CHORDS*

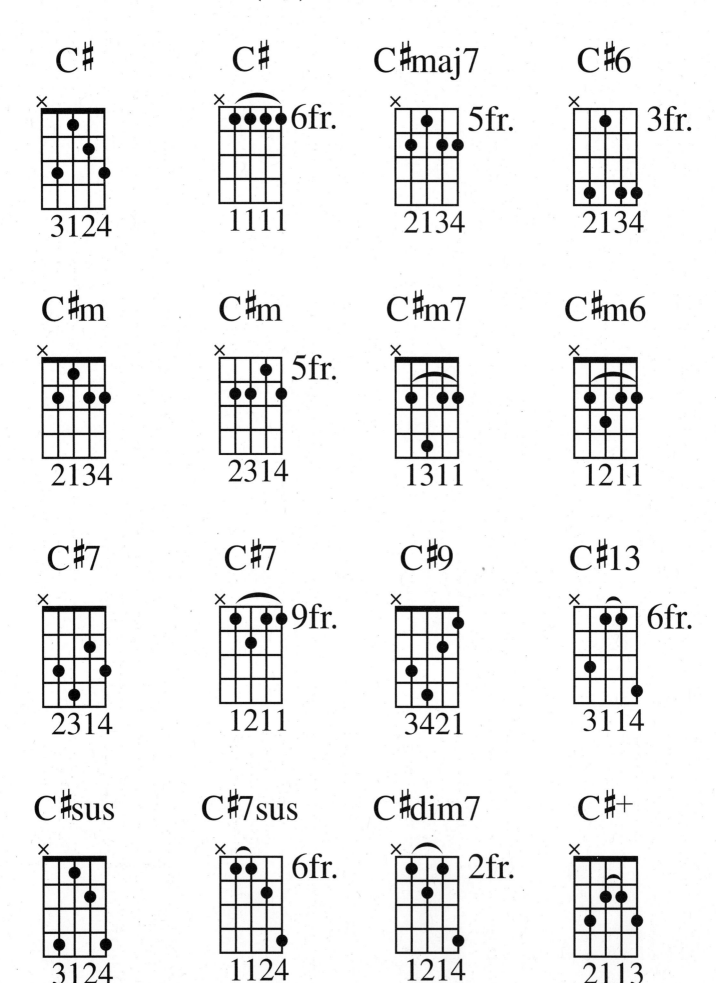

*C♯ and D♭ are two names for the same note.

D CHORDS

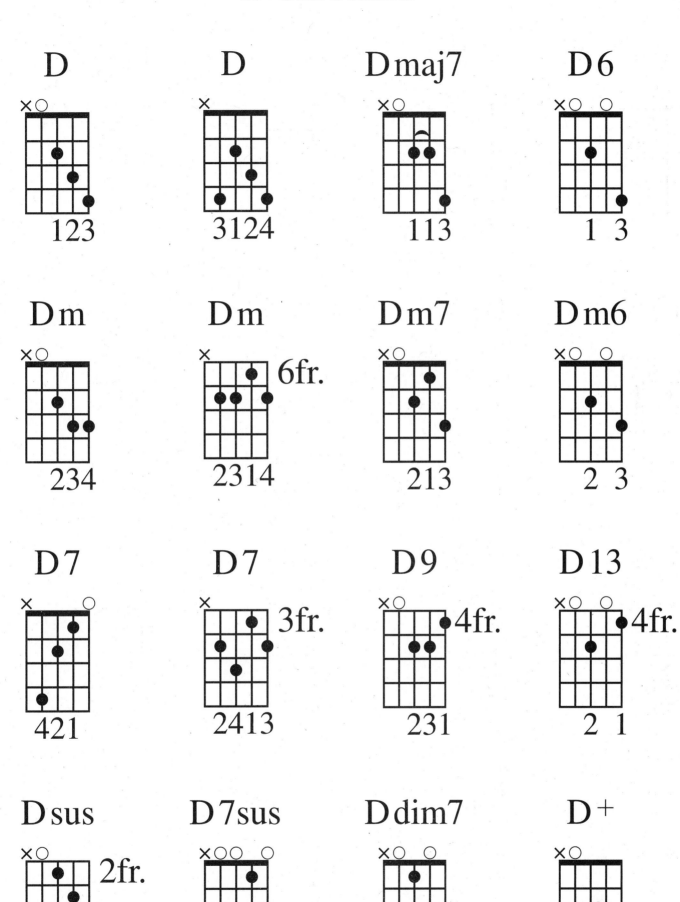

E♭ (D♯) CHORDS*

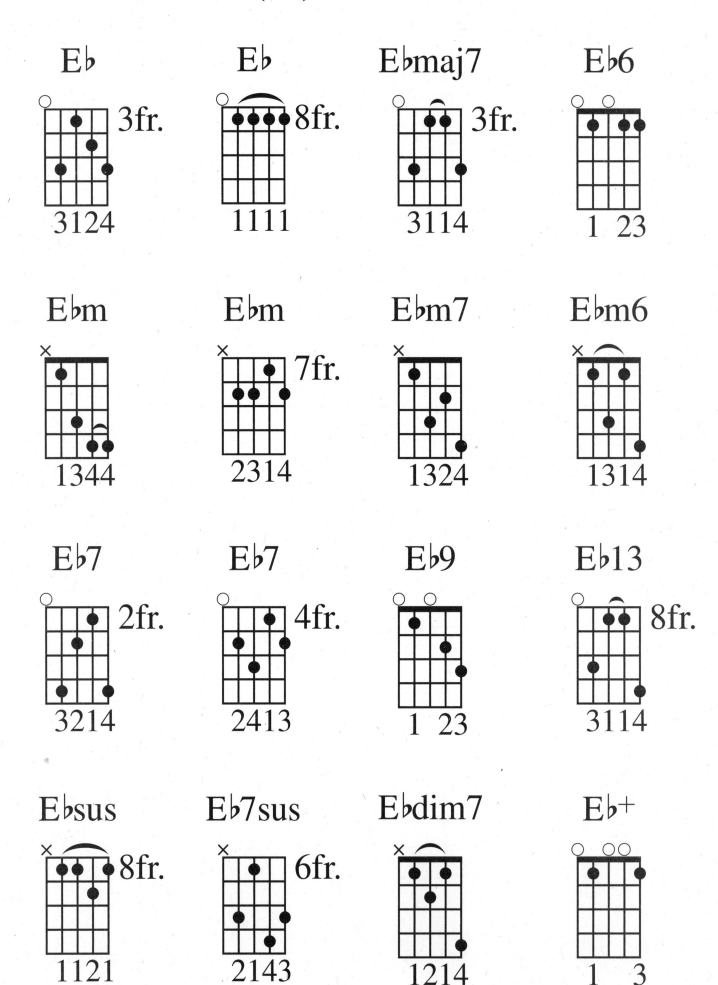

*E♭ and D♯ are two names for the same note.

E CHORDS

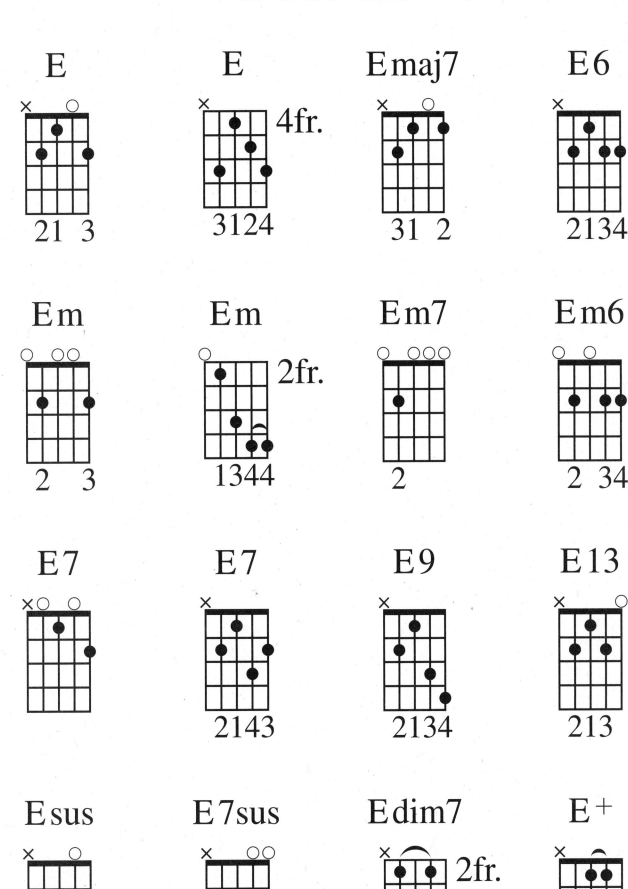

F CHORDS

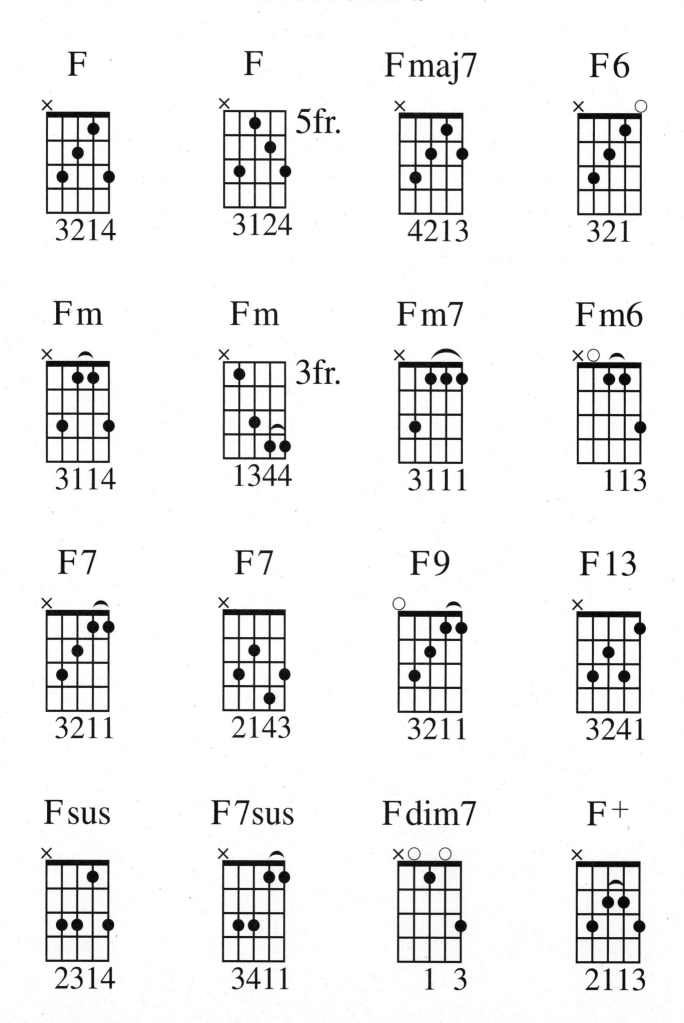

F♯ (G♭) CHORDS*

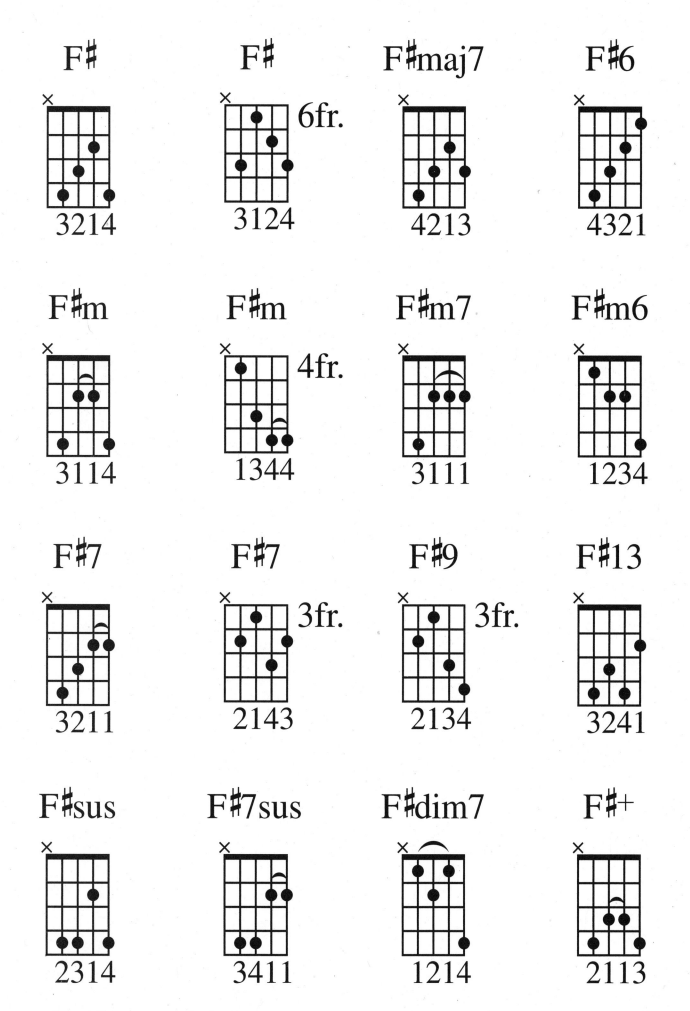

*F♯ and G♭ are two names for the same note.

G CHORDS

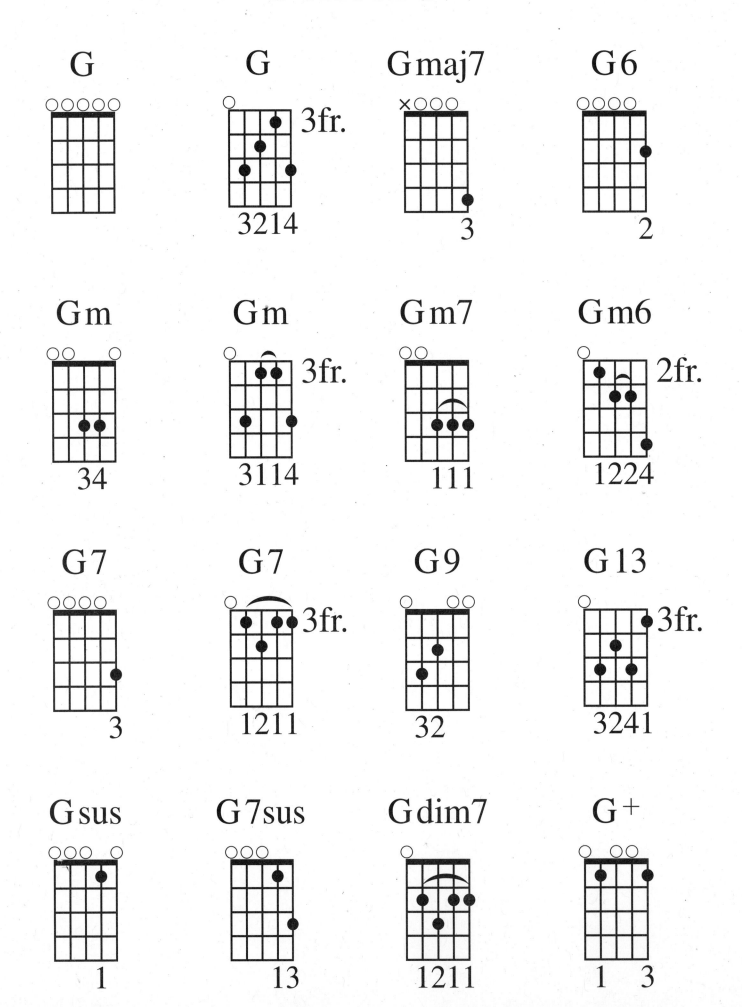

Ab (G#) CHORDS*

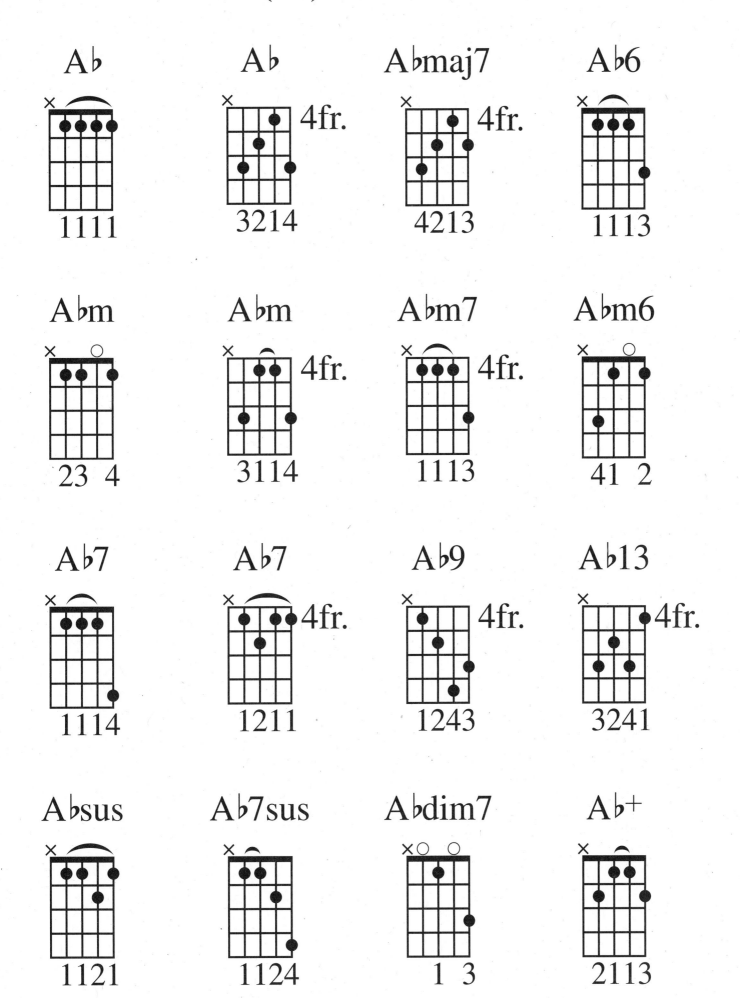

*Ab and G# are two names for the same note.

THE BEST OF
CLASSIC ROCK
GUITAR TAB!

Hotel California
Eagles
(00-24550) Authentic
Guitar TAB, $19.95

**The Very Best
of Eagles**
Eagles
(00-PGM0404) Authentic
Guitar TAB, $34.95

Workingman's Dead
Grateful Dead
(00-PGM0513) Authentic
Guitar TAB, $22.95

Greatest Hits
James Taylor
(00-GF0623) Authentic
Guitar TAB, $22.95

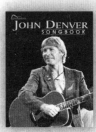
Songbook
John Denver
(00-PGM0113) Authentic
Guitar TAB, $21.95

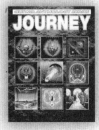
**Guitar Anthology
Series**
Journey
(00-0511B) Authentic
Guitar TAB, $24.95

**Led Zeppelin I–V
(Boxed Set)**
Led Zeppelin
(00-PG9635A) Authentic
Guitar TAB, $99.95

Mothership
Led Zeppelin
(00-30373) Authentic
Guitar TAB, $34.95

Greatest Hits
Mötley Crüe
(00-PGM0309) Authentic
Guitar TAB, $24.95

Cowboys from Hell
Pantera
(00-25955) Authentic
Guitar TAB, $24.95

Guitar TAB Anthology
Pink Floyd
(52-ML1909) Authentic
Guitar TAB, $22.95

The Wall
Pink Floyd
(52-ML2122) Authentic
Guitar TAB, $22.95

**Singles Collection:
The London Years**
Rolling Stones
(00-P0870GTX)
Guitar/TAB/Vocal, $29.95

**Guitar Anthology
Series**
Rush
(00-PG9530) Authentic
Guitar TAB, $24.95

Ultimate Santana
Carlos Santana
(00-29046) Authentic
Guitar TAB, $24.95

**The Best of
Both Worlds**
Van Halen
(00-PGM0418) Authentic
Guitar TAB, $29.95

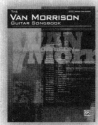
Guitar Songbook
Van Morrison
(00-29972) Authentic
Guitar TAB, $21.95

**Songs You Know by
Heart: Jimmy Buffett's
Greatest Hits**
Jimmy Buffett
(00-P0723GTX) Authentic
Guitar TAB, $18.95

AVAILABLE at YOUR FAVORITE MUSIC RETAILER

Alfred Music Publishing
LEARN · TEACH · PLAY